GERMAN ARMORED TRAINS IN WORLD WAR II

by Wolfgang Sawodny

1469 Morstein Road, West Chester, Pennsylvania 19380

PHOTO CREDITS

—Federal Archives, Koblenz (BA)
—Military Archives, Freiburg (MA)
—Library for History of the Times, Stuttgart (BZ)
—Photo Archives of Prussian Culture, Berlin (PK)
—Imperial War Museum, London (IWM)
—von Alkier Collection, Friedrichsdorf; photos by H. Beckmann (vA)
—Günter Krause Collection, Werl (Kr)
—Edgar Lang (La)
—Podzun Publishers Archives (Po)
—Walter J. Spielberger Collection, Wessling (Sp)
—Dr. Martin Streit, Weilburg (St)

Translated from the German by Dr. Edward Force.

Printed in the United States of America.
ISBN: 0-88740-198-8

This book originally published under the title, "Deutsche Panzerzüge im Zweiten Weltkrieg," Copyright © 1986 by Podzun-Pallas Verlag, 6360 Friedberg 3 (Dorheim). ISBN: 3-7909-0293-4.

ACKNOWLEDGEMENTS

Hearty thanks to Archive Administrator Werner Loos of the Military Archives in Freiburg for his cooperation in the search for information about armored trains, distributed over a wide expanse of documents; to Christian von Alkier and Dipl.-Ing. Günter Krause for their unselfish willingness to place at my disposal the material they had collected on armored trains; to Hans Beckmann, Franz Engelberger, Dr. Martin Streit and Alois Welzel for their patiently provided wealth of information from their own experience; to Edgar Lang and Walter J. Spielberger for additional photographic material; Rainer Rössle for preparing drawings; and to my sons Michael and Oliver for their active help in evaluating material and assembling this book. I would like to thank Messrs. Engelberger and Krause further for their critical examination of the text.

FOREWORD

In the flood of publications on weapons and vehicles of the former German Wehrmacht, one gap has remained until today: until now, hardly anything has been made known about the use of armored trains in World War II. In publications concerning the railroad in the war, armored trains are always mentioned briefly and detachedly, and in the process, many references are erroneous. The pictures provided are usually without explanatory captions. The shortage of informative sources is probably to blame. In the pictorial material, which is rich enough in itself, it is often very difficult to make identifications. The author has been able, through tedious labor, to solve this problem, at least in part, and to attain an impression of the construction and service of the armored trains that, while it still lacks information on some details, is sufficient overall. This is presented for the first time in this volume. Pictures of trains which could not be identified have been included deliberately, in the hope that identification could still be made with the help of readers. The author is presently working on a thorough-going presentation of this material, which is to treat the subject as thoroughly as possible. He would therefore be most grateful for any additions or corrections to his information.

Please send such correspondence to:
Prof. Dr. Wolfgang Sawodny,
Eichenweg 27
D-7915 Elchingen 2, West Germany.

Introduction

After the first railroad train had puffed from Stockton to Darlington, England on September 27, 1825, a military significance of this new means of transportation could have been seen, but it could not have been put into practice until a more or less connected network of tracks had developed in a number of countries. In this respect, the advantages that it offered for troop and supply transport were recognized quite early. The possibility of sending railroad trains directly into battle as weapons took longer to develop. To be sure, the Austrians equipped flatcars with sidewalls of railroad rails to give their marksmen armored protection as early as the revolutionary era of 1848-49, and these cars saw service not only in the siege of Vienna but also in Hungary and northern Italy, and in the American Civil War, Northern as well as Southern states mounted guns on railroad cars, while the French had built armored infantry cars by the end of the Sixties, arming them with mitrailleuses (the forerunners of machine guns), but these were not used in the Franco-Prussian War (1870-71)—though armored railroad batteries, considerably improved over those used in the American Civil War, were built in besieged Paris—but the honor of having built the first genuine armored train in the modern sense—characterized by a blend of infantry and artillery—belongs to the English. It came into being during the Egyptian campaign of 1882. In the following years they often used similar trains in their colonial wars, most frequently (by the end of the war there existed no fewer than 19 such trains) and spectacularly in the Boer War of 1899-1902. From then on, almost all other nations also built armored trains, and until the outbreak of World War II there was scarcely a war in which they did not play a role in one form or another.

The Germans assembled their first armored train in 1904: during the Herero revolt in their colony of Southwest Africa. When World War I began, though, only Russia and Austria owned armored trains (the latter had two at first, later building seven more). The Germans got by (during the mobile war in the west) with makeshift trains at first: boxcars were protected with several layers of sandbags in which loopholes had been left. But soon they too built real armored trains. They were used along with the Austrian ones on the eastern and Balkan fronts throughout the war (and also in northern Italy).—But the real battleground of the armored trains was the former Russian territory after the 1917 revolution. In the partisan battles that followed, all parties, whether Red or White, the Czechs in Siberia, the allied intervention troops, the Finns, Poles or Germans (free corps fighting in the Ukraine before the collapse, and later in the Baltic area), often in massed form, gathered into whole "Armored Train Divisions".

At this time the form of the armored train had developed that was to remain valid into World War II. The combination of infantry and artillery remained decisive. The former were armed with light weapons (including machine guns and grenade throwers) and also included a shock troop that could operate outside the train. Some of the machine guns were built in, and positioned so that they could cover the entire train from the sides as well as from elevated positions (remember that the trains might stand in cuts or on causeways), so they could drive off an enemy approach. The preferred artillery was light-caliber guns (mostly 7.5 to 10.5 cm), generally built in rotating turrets with a turning range of at least 270 degrees. All the cars were armored as was the locomotive, usually only against small-caliber guns and shrapnel, to keep the weight down. The cars were arranged as symmetrically as possible around the locomotive running in the middle (often equipped with an auxiliary tender to increase its range), with the infantry wagons and command wagon closest in, the latter equipped with telephone and radio communication within the train and outside, then the artillery wagons, so the guns could be brought into action pointing either inward or outward. At the head and tail of the train were so-called "controllers" or pusher cars; they were supposed to push away mines lying on the track or "fire cars" pushed toward the train (for example, boxcars filled with explosives), to prevent them from harming the train. They were also loaded with track-laying materials, with which the engineer unit traveling on the train could repair track damage that hindered the train's movement. For armor they usually had just an armored trolley or a scout car with railroad wheels for reconnaissance purposes, as well as a supply and repair train which was stationed at the depot that served as the armored train's base of operations. Thus the armored train was a complete unit in itself, which could operate independently. There were considerable variations in size and strength: the Czechs preferred very small trains with just one artillery car before and one infantry car behind the locomotive; the Russians and Poles had very powerful trains with at least

3

four heavy guns. Accordingly, the number of the crew could vary strongly too—between 40 and 200 men, with the average being roughly company strength.

There was a wide variety of possible uses of armored trains:

Independent offensive battle assignments:
a) Reconnaissance along the track, especially of railway facilities (stations, bridges, tunnels etc.)
b) Taking possession of railway facilities.
c) Invasion of enemy territory.
d) Offensive intervention in battles.
e) Artillery action aimed at targets from advanced positions.
f) Pursuit (and perhaps capture) of retreating enemy forces.

Independent defensive assignments:
a) Blocking enemy advances.
b) (Surprise) counterattacks against advancing enemy forces.
c) Fighting off enemy armored columns.
d) Rear-guard protection of withdrawals.
e) Rounding up retreating troop units.
f) Fighting off enemy raids on rear transport lines.
g) Coastal defense.

Support assignments:
a) Supporting infantry attacks and defenses through use of weapons, especially artillery.
b) Flank protection of units operating parallel to railway lines.
c) Leading attacks by moving against hindrances in the terrain.
d) Artillery battle from concealed positions.
e) Radio coordination of operations by mixed battle groups.

Securing assignments:
a) Guarding and replacing railway facilities.
b) Guarding communication lines to the rear.
c) Guarding troop concentrations.
d) Guarding supply depots.
e) Guarding transport of troops and supplies during transportation and unloading.
f) Patrolling railway lines.

During the Thirties, to be sure, much doubt was cast on the further utility of armored trains, as they were bound to the network of railway lines, offered a relatively large target, and were expensive to create and maintain. The much smaller and more mobile armored wheeled and tracked vehicles seemed to be far superior to them for fighting purposes. There was also the threat of air attack, in which not only direct hits but bombing of the tracks before and behind the train could paralyze it. For that reason the Poles developed the concept of numerous armored trolleys, which could operate independently as needed or in groups, could protect a greater expense of track, and when coupled together could concentrate more firepower than armored trains could. But this concept did not develop beyond the testing stage before the war began.

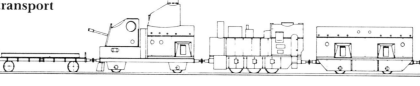

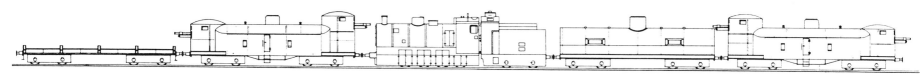

Prewar types of armored trains: Czech (ex-Austro-Hungarian) armored train with minimal equipment (above); train armed with more artillery, as was preferred in Poland and the Soviet Union (below).

From the Outbreak of the War to the Summer of 1941

With the disbanding of the free corps at the beginning of the Twenties, the last armored trains also disappeared from German rails. But not for long; it was no later than 1929-30 that the German Railways set up so-called "track-guarding trains" to protect the railway network during internal unrest. They consisted of lightly armored locomotives of Series 57 and 93 (former Prussian G10 and T14) and externally scarcely changed boxcars that had been made somewhat impervious by having double walls of railroad track or cement placed behind their outer walls. Twenty-two such trains existed in 1937.

During the Thirties, the German military command had come to regard armored trains as weapons superseded by the development of aircraft and armored units, and thus saw no reason to build them. Only shortly before the outbreak of war (in July and August of 1939) did they change their minds and decide to set up seven armored trains after all. In the short time available, only makeshift solutions were possible: they made use of the locomotives and cars of the track-guarding trains plus the armored trains seized in Czechoslovakia. As a result, the fighting strength of these trains— despite being manned by goodly numbers of infantrymen—could not be regarded as very high, especially as the 7.5-cm guns were mounted in casemates with limited arcs of aim. Yet they remained in service until the autumn of 1944 with the exception of Train No. 5, which was mustered out in the summer of 1940; naturally, they were often rebuilt and improved.

At first the critics of armored trains seemed to be right. Attempts to capture railroad bridges unharmed with their help failed, as far as was reported (at Dirschau in the Polish campaign and Arnheim in Holland). They also supplied protective service, as for example in the upper Rhine Valley.—Before the French campaign began, three more armored trains (No. 23 to 25) had been established, composed of the same railway protection and Czech rolling stock as the earlier ones (No. 1 to 7). The guns (likewise 7.5-cm cannon made by the Skoda firm) were often still mounted in casements, and in Train No. 24 even on open cars, from which they had to fire over the armored sides ("over the banks"). All three trains were taken out of service on October 2, 1940, unlike two captured Polish armored trains, which joined the Wehrmacht in June and July of 1940 as No. 21 and 22. These two powerful battle units (No. 22 was armed with three 7.5-cm 02/26(p) guns), No. 21 with two 10-cm 14/19(p) light F.H. as well, all in rotating turrets) moved into occupied France in April of 1941.

Before the Russian campaign began, Armored Trains No. 23 and 24 were reactivated. To be sure, they were sent to see service in Serbia, where partisans were already making the railroad lines unsafe. The plan of attacking the Soviet Union, though, posed a further problem: Russia did not use the normal gauge (1435 mm) of Central Europe, but a broad gauge of 1524 mm. The earlier armored trains thus could not be used on the Russian railway lines, or at best only in the hinterlands after refitting.

Locomotive (series 57) of an early armored train (No. 1-7). The complicated armor, suited to the form of the train, offered many bullet traps despite its angling. (BA)

In order to have armored trains available near the front too, the trains had to be built to broad gauge. On May 28, 1941 the OKH ordered appropriate refitting for trains 26 to 31. This again came so late that only makeshift solutions were possible. For the infantry, open freight cars were fitted with low steel walls for shot protection. Each train had one (No. 30 and 31) or two (No. 26-29) of these cars, as well as two (No. 29-31) or three (No. 26-28) Somua S 35 tanks captured in France, likewise open cars, with side armor to protect the running gear of tanks that were loaded on them. Artillery was not available. The trains were pulled by series 57 (G10) locomotives (only No. 29 had a WR 550 D Diesel locomotive), a number of which had been rebuilt for broad gauge, in order to keep things moving on Russian tracks—before enough captured material was available). They had only cab armor.

At the beginning of the Russian campaign, the armored trains at this front were divided as follows (division among battle groups is definite, as to armies, at least numerically correct):

	Normal Gauge	Broad Gauge	Stationed at
North Group:			
18th Army	No. 6		Insterburg
16th Army		No. 26 & 30	Eydtkau
Middle Group:			
9th Army	No. 1 & 3		Ortelsburg
4th Army	No. 2	No. 28 & 29	Warsaw, Terespol, Platerow
2nd Armored Group		No. 27	Terespol
South Group:			
6th Army	No. 4 & 7		Kielce
17th Army		No. 31	Zurawica

Photos of the earlier armored trains (No. 1-7) are rare. They show the generous use of freight cars from the former track-guarding trains. In Armored Train No. 3 of Munich (above), the front part of the armored superstructure with the gun could be rotated to a limited degree. Notice too the large loopholes in the armor. The Dresden Tarin No. 2 (below) has a rotating turret. (BA/MA, photos by Ollenschläger)

Left: As early as the spring of 1940 the artillery cars of Armored Train No. 3 (previous page) were rebuilt and equipped with a rotating turret open at the top, in which an experimental 7.5-cm L/41 gun with muzzle brake, a forerunner of the Pak 40, was installed. (IWM)

Pictures below: Armored Train No. 22, assembled from captured Polish rolling stock, in France (probably in 1942). Behind the artillery car with its two 7.5-cm guns is another boxcar for the infantry. The right picture shows a 2-cm anti-aircraft gun on the front pusher car (with armored low walls). (2 x BA)

Left: the rear part of Armored Train No. 22, which is being inspected by a commanding general: this artillery car carries only one 7.5-cm gun (note the machine-gun port); in front of it is the command car with the antenna running around the roof. (BA)

Further details of Armored Train 22. Left: Before the rotating turret of the forward artillery car is a 2-cm anti-aircraft gun on an armored flatcar. Above: Along with the 2-cm anti-aircraft gun, twinned machine guns in sliding roof hatches could also be used for defense against aircraft.

Right: The locomotive, of Polish series Ti 3 (ex-Prussian G5[1]) had an armored observation post for the engineer on the tender. The attachment of the armored aprons is also easy to see. (3 x BA)

Armored Train No. 23 in service in the Balkans (1941/42). Before and behind the locomotive (No. 93,220) are auxiliary boxcars, but the train also includes armored infantry cars. On the pusher car (far right) is a trolley. While the forward artillery car has a rotating turret, the rear cannon (at left) is still housed in a casemate in a car that comes from an Austro-Hungarian armored train of World War II (probably reaching the Wehrmacht as Czech or Polish booty). (2 x BA)

While most armored trains scarcely changed their areas of service, Train No. 24, which these pictures show in Italy after thorough rebuilding, traveled far: the Balkans in 1941-43, Italy in the spring of 1944, France in the summer of 1944, the eastern front as of the autumn of 1944.

Left: Despite the completed rebuilding, the 7.5-cm guns are still mounted open on platforms and have to shoot over the boards. On another raised platform is the 2-cm anti-aircraft gun; the armored observation tower between them and the spotlight are easy to see. Below: The crew disembarks from the forward half of the train. The Series 57 locomotive still has the close armor, but all the infantry cars are genuine armored cars, though of different types. Lower right: Armored Train No. 24 certainly had removable 38(t) tanks at this time, but on temporarily reequipped flatcars without loading ramps. The tanks had to be removed, when necessary, by the crew, using planks carried on the train. (3 x BA)

Pictures of a German armored train that has to date not been identified definitely. The artillery cars are of Polish origin (compare with the captured train, above right), which suggests that this is one of the trains known to have been assembled out of such materials (No. 10, 11 or 21), which, however, were not active in the area shown in the pictures (Minsk). (3 BA, 1 Pk)

Above:
These few pictures do not indicate which armored train is shown. The four-axle artillery car with two guns is doubtless captured from Russia or Poland.

Below:
Armored Train No. 30, after the addition of captured Russian cars and armor-bearing cars, and with broad-gauge wheels (German G10 locomotive) in 1943.
(BA)

Summer of 1941 to the End of 1942

The fact that the armored trains were usually thought of only at the last second and then usually could only be equipped in a makeshift way, was attributable to the unfavorable conditions. The building and equipping were to be done on the orders of the OKH by the IN 10 (Railroad Engineers) of the General Army Office in cooperation with appropriate branches of the Army Weapons Office (particularly WuG 5 and 6). As for a crew, the armored train was assigned to a particular war zone. The crew, at best only of company strength, was gathered from the most varied troop units (infantry, artillery, anti-aircraft, railroad engineers, intelligence, smoke-screen and sanitary units), generally volunteers, which had as much effect on quick teamwork as did the replacement situation. The technical crew of an armored train (a railroad inspector as technical leader of the train, two drivers, three firemen, two track watchmen, and one motor and lighting serviceman, simultaneously wagonmaster) were, moreover, provided on demand via the transport services of the Federal Transportation Ministry, by the German Railway for the duration of the war.

After equipping and manning, the armored train, as a battle group, moved to the jurisdiction of the OKH, which ordered it to serve with appropriate troop units.— Naturally, the Railroad Engineers had no particular interest in a weapon that they had to prepare but that was then taken away from their influence; and in the OKH a special unit, that numbered fewer than 2000 men in all, and whose value was in dispute as well, could only have a marginal effect.

After these last-moment makeshift solutions in the auxiliary Armored Trains 26 to 31 had caused particularly bad results, help was finally provided. As ordered on August 9, 1941, the armored trains were turned over to the fast-moving forces, and under their weapons-general the position of a staff officer for armored railway trains was created to command the troops serving on them. From the beginning until its dissolution on March 31, 1945 this position was held by Lieutenant Colonel (later Colonel) Egon von Olszewski. Thanks to his energy and organizational talents, the armored trains were to experience a considerable development in the following years. But concrete effects were seen only as of 1942.

The Russians—traditionally inclined to use armored trains and equipped with plenty of them—were first to demonstrate that these weapons definitely had their merits in defensive action. Of course many were put out of action by the effects of German aircraft, artillery and tanks, but on the southern front in particular, where numbers of them often went into battle together in the manner of "armored train divisions", they caused the German troops much trouble and stopped, with lasting effect, the advances of Armored Group 1 on Rostov in the late autumn of 1941.

It is not surprising that a whole series of Russian trains were captured during the German advance, what with so many in action at the front. They were soon put to use on the German side. Reequipping the broad-gauge No. 26 to 31 was especially easy; adding Russian armored locomotives and armored artillery cars (with two to four 7.62-cm 295/l(r) field guns) rid them of their auxiliary status. Other German armored trains were also upgraded similarly; for example, No. 6 was armored and given captured Russian cars with four such guns. Additional material was utilized by the German battle troops as well as those on guard behind the lines, using their own means to produce a series of auxiliary armored trains that were not subordinated to the OKH or the staff officer of armored railroad trains, but remained under the command of the units that had produced them. (To avoid confusion, they could, as ordered by the OKH on July 12, 1943, only be called "track-guarding trains".) Naturally, the equipment and crews of these trains varied very much. Often they were nothing but boxcars armored in makeshift fashion with sandbags, cement walls etc., and armed only with infantry weapons (antitank guns, grenade throwers, machine guns), though there were also trains that had considerable firepower through the use of captured artillery cars or installation of Russian tank turrets on cars. Naming the track-guarding trains varied greatly; one finds numbers as well as letters, names of people ("Blücher", "Rübezahl"), first names ("Max", "Werner") or place names ("Zobten", "Berlin", "Stettin"). Sometimes it happened that such trains were included in the list of official armored trains: on June 16, 1942 the auxiliary train "Stettin" or "A" (with four 4.5-cm KwK in Russian BT-7 tank turrets) was made Armored Train No. 51; on February 10, 1944 the track-guarding train "R" was taken over without changing its designation, and on June 1, 1944 the track-guarding train "Blücher" became Armored Train No. 52. In March of 1945, in view of the lack of sufficient new construction, a whole series of these trains were made official in one stroke ("Berlin", "Max", "Moritz", "Werner", No. 83 and No. 350). Auxiliary armored trains also appeared in areas where no official ones were stationed, for example in Norway (the trains "Norwegen", "Voss", "Grong" and "Narvik").

Along with the rebuilt trains and the aforementioned No. 51, only two other regular armored trains reached the troops in 1942. In the winter of 1941/42, Armored Train No. 25, out of service for more than a year, was reactivated. It was sent to France in exchange for Armored Train No. 21, which was sent in November of 1942 to the 9th (later 2nd) Army on the eastern front. In January of 1942 the South Army Group put a broad-gauge unit made up of captured Polish and Russian rolling stock into service; following the pattern of Russian armored train divisions, it consisted of two battle trains (each with four 7.5- or 10-cm caliberguns), No. 10a and 10b. This unit, to be sure, does not seem to have proved itself. In August of 1943 it was divided; No. 10a remained No. 10, and 10b became a separate Armored Train No. 11.

To the photos:
At the beginning of war with the Soviet Union, provisional broad-gauge trains (No. 26 to 31) were built hastily, scarcely deserving the name "armored train". For the infantry there were only flatcars with low armored sides, which offered protection only to men lying down. The artillery amounted to the 4.7-cm guns of the captured Somua S-35 tanks carried on flatcars. In this train (No. 29) there is not even any protection for the running gear of the tank. Behind the tank-carrying car is the diesel locomotive (WR 550 D), the only one Train NO. 29 had. (2 x BA)

At the beginning of the Russian campaign, the Germans hoped to capture so many locomotives and cars so quickly that rail traffic could keep running on the Russian broad-gauge tracks. Despite the quick advance during the first months, this hope was not to come true. The Russians were able to move their rolling stock far away and destroy the network of track as well as the technical facilities as they retreated. For that reason, the Germans began to change the tracks to normal gauge quickly and in an ever-expanding area, so that they could use the tracks for German trains. Naturally, this also allowed the quick deployment of the normal-gauge armored trains stationed on the eastern front (No. 1-4, 6 & 7) in the conquered areas. In the summer of 1942, even all the broad-gauge armored trains (No. 10 and 26-31) were converted to normal gauge.

This is surprising, insofar as the offensive moving straight ahead in the southern area of the eastern front would lead them to expect a considerable increase in broad-gauge tracks. The assumptions were presumably made that an offensive use of the armored trains was not advisable in any case, that a quick changing of the tracks would be possible, and that the area near the front could be protected by auxiliary trains in the interim.

The division of the armored trains as 1941 became 1942 was like that at the beginning of the war, except that now they were stationed far inside the enemy's country: With the Northern Army Group, No. 30 was behind the Leningrad front, No. 6 in the Dno-Novgorod region, and No. 26 between Novosokolniki and Dno; with the Central Army Group, No. 1 and 2 were in the Polozk-Orscha-Witebsk-Smolensk area, No. 27, 28

and 29 in the Brjansk-Orel-Kursk region; with the Southern Army Group, No. 4 was between Dnepropetrovsk and Saporoshje, No. 31 between Krementschug and Poltava, the newly arrived Armored Train No. 10 was in service at Darnitza (on the east shore of the Dniepr near Kiev). No. 3 and 7 were in the hinterlands for repairs. For the rest of 1942 there are no individual data available, but only indications of how the trains were divided among the army groups:

```
1/1/1942 6/15/1942 8/7/1942 10/8/1942
Northern    1N & 2B   1N & 1B   2N   3N
Central     2N & 3B   3N   4N   5N
Southern (A&B)  1N & 2B   2N & 3B   1N & 3B*   4N
N: Normal gauge, B: Broad gauge *: Gauge changed
```

In addition to the process of changing the gauge, one also notes a transfer of trains to the Southern Army Group before the start of their summer offensive and thereafter a slow increase with the Central Army Group, caused by the constantly increasing activity of Russian partisans in its rear zone. In securing the track network, protecting the troop and supply trains using it, and actively fighting partisans, the armored trains took on important tasks which kept them ever busier in the following period and made their

The tank-carrying car of Train No. 28, with armored side aprons. The loading ramp for the tank was folded up when the train was in motion and stowed on the pusher car ahead. (BA)

15

Above: Armored Train No. 28 at full size. Trains 26 through 28 had three tank-carrying cars with Somua S 35 tanks. The artillery cars could—what a luxury!—even be covered with a canvas canopy—at least to keep off rain. The Type 57 locomotive, converted to broad gauge, had only temporary cab armor. (BA)

Below:
It is hard to believe that this is the same Armored Train No. 28--after being equipped with captured Russian material in the early summer of 1942. In the background are the tank-carrying cars retained from the original train, with the Somua S 35 tanks. (BA)

necessity more and more obvious. Though the armored trains are mentioned only briefly and generally in the OKW directive for fighting partisans on November 11, 1942, there is—based on experience—a whole section devoted to them in the volume "Fighting Partisans" of the OKW of May 6, 1944, from which informative information about their activities in this area can be gained. Most indicative of the unique nature of the armored trains is their use in large-scale operations against partisans (by advances with independent fighting orders, participation with disembarkable units, blocking the partisans' retreat paths across the railway lines, providing artillery support or serving as command posts for the attacking staff) and carrying out small-scale independent operations (as pursuit commands). Other tasks include: intervention in attacks on transports and attempts to damage railway lines, securing moves with appropriate secrecy and camouflage, escort firepower for important transport, courier and special trains, track maintenance at rail intersections where fighting is going on, assistance in successful attacks, securing threatened railway facilities, and work on or near the tracks, transport of infantry units (up to column strength under armor in the train itself, beyond that in added cars), distribution of propaganda material.

The securing of communication lines to the rear against flank attacks by regular Russian troops was also necessary, for example, the essential Smolensk-Wiasma-Sytschevka-Rshev line, needed to maintain the front lines at Rshev (protected in part by hurriedly assembled auxiliary armored trains) in the first months of 1942, or the maintenance of the 83rd I.D., situated alone in the wide valley of Welikije Luki, in the summer of 1942 (by Armored Trains No. 3 and 28).

In view of this increasing significance, the establishment in the summer of 1941 of a troop-serving central office with the staff officer of armored trains under the general of the fast-moving troops in the OKH was especially helpful. His activities showed their first visible effects in the spring of 1942. On April 1, 1942 the Railway Armor Replacement Department was established in Warsaw-Rembertov (belonging to Defensive Area I), where assembling, construction, replacement, repair and servicing of armored trains was done by a single agency after its successful establishment by In 6 and 10 of the AHA. On May 24, 1942 the general of the fast-moving troops distributed the "Temporary Guidelines for Assembly and Utilization of Armored Trains" prepared by the staff officer of armored trains. But most important was the conceptualization of an armored train as a unit of battle strength, which proved itself so well that it was produced until the war's end with only minor modifications.

Additional pictures of the reequipped Armored Train No. 28.

Above: A second captured artillery car with 7.62-cm cannon behind the locomotive. Lower left: Stopping at a station. The locomotive is a captured O-series machine, the most commonly used armored locomotive on the Soviet side. Lower right: This picture clearly shows the lashings of the Somua tank. In the foreground is the folded loading ramp, carried on the pusher car. (3 x BA)

Another broad-gauge armored train made of captured Russian rolling stock. Its being armed with four guns (though by the thickness of their barrels they are smaller than the usual 7.62-cm caliber) shows it to be a regular armored train, perhaps of the reequipped 26-31 series, but a more precise identification based on this pictorial material is impossible for the time being. (3 x BA)

An auxiliary broad-gauge armored train (track-guarding train), manned by the 3rd Company of Railroad Engineer Regiment No. 3 in Kleist's armored unit (Southern Army Group), consisting of a Russian Type O armored locomotive (upper right), a captured two-turret artillery car, from which one cannon has been removed (lower left), and three low-board cars (with doubled walls of cast concrete or piled sandbags), manned by infantrymen, with a 3.7-cm antitank gun in front (lower right). (3 BA, 1 La).

The broad-gauge armored train "Polko" was likewise powered by a Russian Type O armored locomotive. While the double anti-aircraft machine guns are housed in an auxiliary octagonal turret (upper left), the well-armed artillery car has two T-34 turrets with their effective 7.62-cm KwK. (3 x BA)

At the Roslavl yards in April of 1942, this imposing captured Russian armored locomotive (the picture at lower left shows the German cross painted over the Russian star) is put back into service. Unfortunately, the type cannot be recognized, nor is it known which armored train it was part of. (3 x BA)

Deutsche Wehrmacht

A remarkable track-guarding train in the Mediterranean area, presumably southern France. The foreign (French?) 1C locomotive with cab armor is coupled to a German (G 10?) tender. The use of a passenger car in an armored train is very unusual.

Pictures below: The armored infantry cars are secured at the bottom with a double layer of crossties to protect against mines. The tanks carried are a Hotchkiss H 39 (lower left) and three ancient Renault FT 17. (3 x BA)

Pictures of other track-guarding trains with guns mounted on top of boxcars. Trolleys running at the front can be seen above. Right: So-called disembarking boxes, handy for disembarking from the floor of the car, with some cars carrying machine gunners. (2 BA, 1 IWM).

At times track-guarding trains were upgraded to regular armored trains, like this one early in 1942, formerly called "A" or "Stettin", now Armored Train No. 51. The artillery cars are rebuilt boxcars with Russian BT-7 tank turrets, built in stepped form so that both 4.5-cm cannon can be deployed to the front at once. After the anti-aircraft car behind the locomotive was a second artillery wagon, just like the first. (2 St, 1 vA)

Armored Train Units BP42 and BP44, and Armored Scout Cars and Railcars

For the armored train units of Type BP42 (not EP42, as has been stated in previous literature), the artillery was increased, following Russian and Polish examples, to four guns, which were not, though, mounted two to a car as in the latter types, but one per separately built ten-sided rotating turret, in order to avoid too-great losses from a direct hit. The two halves of the train, before and behind the locomotive (usually of Series 57 (G10)) were identical and consisted of (from the locomotive out) one artillery car with one 10-cm-le.F.H. 14/19(p) gun, one command and infantry car and one artillery and anti-aircraft car with one 7.62-cm F.K. 295/1(r) and one 2-cm anti-aircraft quadruple unit (though there were also trains in which all four guns were of the same type—either 7.62 or 10 mm). All the cars were covered with angled armor (15 to 30 mm), which also covered the running gear. The locomotives too, unlike the earlier ones with their customary "skin-tight" complex armor with many corners that caught shells, were covered with a smooth-surfaced armor some distance away from the vehicle itself, which not only offered passage behind the armor but also afforded better protection.

Though the Armored Trains No. 26-31 were very primitive as set up at the beginning of the Russian campaign, one of their facilities proved itself well: the tanks carried on flatcars and quickly unloaded via loading ramps, which considerably strengthened the battle group operating outside the train (at first only infantry, sometimes with bicycles), and expanded their range of operation significantly. So two such tank-carrying cars with tanks, generally of the Praga 38 (t) type, with 3.7-cm KwK guns and two machine guns, were also included in the BP42 armored trains.—The reconnaissance vehicles too—formerly an armored but unarmed trolley and a railroad-wheeled motorcycle—were upgraded. Every BP42 unit was given, in place of these, two Panhard 38(f) (P 204) armored scout cars with 2.5-cm KwK guns and one machine gun, which could be used both on rails and—after a ten-minute wheel change—on roads. Some of the older armored trains were gradually equipped with such removable tanks and Panhard scout cars too.

With the BP42 a unit had been created that was well equipped for infantry and partisan warfare. But since, from 1943 on, the armored trains were exposed more and more to Russian attacks with many tanks, they revealed a vulnerable spot. While they themselves offered a large and easily vulnerable target, they could scarcely provide equal firepower, even with their artillery armament. For that reason, BP42 to BP44 were developed further. After they reached the fronts at the German borders, interruptions caused by breaking of the rail network were naturally to be expected, and the armored trains could provide almost exclusively defensive use, which meant that the pusher cars at the ends of the train seemed dispensable. They were replaced by cars on which Panzer IV turrets with 7.5 cm KwK L/48 guns were mounted, the so-called armored pursuit cars. The 10.5-cm 18M field howitzer was now mounted (in the same turret as in BP42)/ In addition, to increase effectiveness, a reorganization of the crew (without increasing numbers by much) was carried out. The transition from BP42 to BP44 presumably took place with Armored Train No. 73 (the first documented train of Type BP44) in the spring of 1944, but toward the war's end, the lack of materials became more and more obvious, so that—especially in the last months—one had to use what was at hand and improvise. No longer were captured 7.62 and 10-cm guns used, and above all, not enough armored pursuit cars were available. For these reasons, the originally planned reequipping of the still available Type BP 42 trains with these cars could not be done; instead, some of the earlier armored trains (No. 1-31) were equipped with BP42 cars during 1943 and 1944.

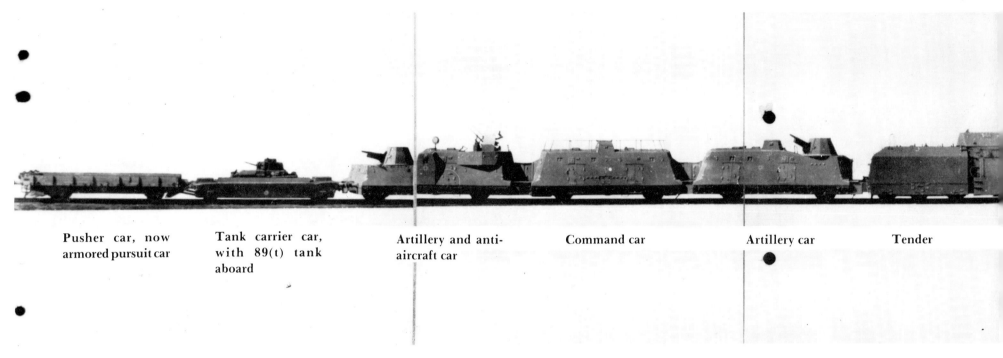

| Pusher car, now armored pursuit car | Tank carrier car, with 89(t) tank aboard | Artillery and anti-aircraft car | Command car | Artillery car | Tender |

The model of the standard armored train of Type BP 42. It remained with only minor modifications (changing the pusher cars to armored pursuit cars by adding Panzer IV turrets and replacing captured guns with le.F.H. 18M), as the further development, BP 44. (BA)

In 1943 the concept was taken up that had been debated before the war, especially in Poland, but that had its proponents in Germany too: motor-driven, armed and armored trolleys that could be used singly, in groups of several individual vehicles, or coupled together as one train. Heightened flexibility and greater mobility were expected from such units. From these considerations there arose the armored railroad trains (le.Sp.) and (s.Sp.) (Sp. = Spähwagen, scout car). The armored train (light scout car) consisted of ten railroad-wheeled armored scout cars in all, each driven by an air-cooled 76-HP Steyr motor (top speed 70 kph), armed with four light machine guns, a six-man crew, 14.5-mm armor and a gross weight of 8 tons. It was well suited to securing the tracks, especially against partisans, but was not usable in other battle tasks because of its lack of any heavy weapons. For that reason, only four such units were made (No. 301-304), which were supplied to troops in the Balkans in the spring of 1944. — The armored train (heavy scout car) consisted of twelve rail-wheeled armored scout cars with varying equipment: one command car (company, troop, radio and medical personnel), one tactical car for the infantry column (troops, built-in machine gun), two infantry cars (each with one built-in machine gun, plus a total of one heavy and four light machine guns and two 8-cm grenade throwers), one engineer car (one built-in and two additional machine guns, flame-thrower); one tactical car for the artillery column (one machine gun), four gun cars with Panzer III/N or IV turrets and short 7.5-cm KwK L/24 (toward the end of the war, two of these cars were armed with 8- or 12-cm grenade throwers because of a lack of tank turrets), two anti-aircraft cars with quadruple 2-cm guns (in the first trains, also 3.7-cm twin anti-aircraft guns). At the ends of the train there were also tank-carrying cars with Praga 38(t) tanks and pusher cars, as well as a Panhard 38(f) scout car as a reconnaissance vehicle. The individual armored scout cars had 20-mm

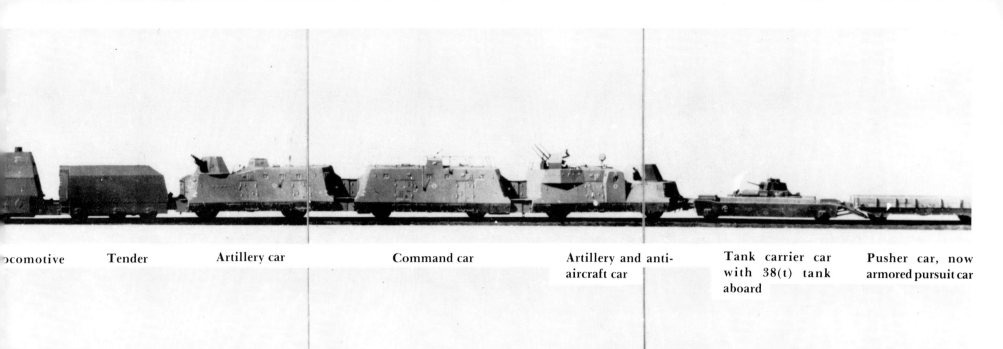

| ocomotive | Tender | Artillery car | Command car | Artillery and anti-aircraft car | Tank carrier car with 38(t) tank aboard | Pusher car, now armored pursuit car |

armor and a gross weight of about 18 tons (varying depending on equipment). They were powered by the same 76-HP Steyr motors as the lighter vehicles. Because of this weak powerplant, the heavy scout cars could only attain a speed of 40 kph. All in all, the fighting power of the heavy armored trains approximately equaled that of the BP42, but the mobile infantry unit was, with 25 men, only half as great, yet the range (with speed cut to 20 kph) was almost quadrupled to 700 kilometers. It is not known whether the trains that saw service had a reduced number of cars because of the prevailing lack of materials. The fact that every car had its own motor was a great advantage; no longer could a direct hit on the locomotive cripple the whole train. The possible applications were also more numerous: the infantry cars could be placed farther forward, the gun cars farther back as an infantry-supporting battery and

thus less exposed to enemy action. Although ten heavy armored trains were planned for the first half of 1944, the first two (No. 201 and 202) only reached the troops in the Balkans in November of 1944. No. 203 and 204 followed in January of 1945. Numbers 205 through 208 were subsequently built, but it is possible that not all of them saw service; the construction of No. 209 and 210 was cancelled as of January 1945.

Along with the armored trains, there were also armored railcars as individual units. Apparently there were fifteen such vehicles when the war began, armed only with machine guns. All but one must have been out of service by the summer of 1940. But Railcar No. 15, on the other hand, can be documented until the end of the war. The building of Armored Railcar No. 16 was completed only on December 29, 1942. It was a large vehicle with two 7.62-cm FK 295/l(r)

guns in rotating turrets like those of BP 42. It fell into Polish hands and is today a museum piece at the Skarzysko-Kamienna railroad station. A similar but somewhat smaller vehicle captured from the Russians—likewise with two 7.62-cm guns in rotating turrets— had been put into service earlier (December 1943) as Armored Railcar No. 17. Whether the similar subsequent railcar No. 18 to 23 (begun on March 3, 1943, finished in November 1943 (No. 21-23) or January 1944 (No. 21-23), all of which reached the troops only in the latter half of 1944) were all likewise of Russian origin or at least partly German copies is not clear. Along with the two aforementioned guns, these railcars had four machine guns, 21-man crews and 20-mm armor; their gross weight amounted to 34 tons, and an eight-cylinder 180-HP motor gave them a top speed of 60 kph (with a range of 500 km). Aside from the independently

Two pictures showing the complete BP 42 standard armored train. In the picture below, it is presumably Train No. 61, the first of this type, which reached the troops at the end of 1942. (BA, vA)

operation Railcar No. 15, equipped with only machine guns, all the other aforementioned armored trains were divided up to provide welcome strengthening of artillery and also carried out reconnaissance and other assignments. In the spring the Italian firm of Ansaldo-Fossati was contracted with to produce nine armored railcars (Littorine blindate) of Type ALn-56. of which they had already delivered five units to the Italian Army, for the German Wehrmacht (Railcars NO. 30-38). They had two Italian M 1ì0 tank turrets with 4.7-cm KwK, a 2-cm anti-aircraft gun (Breda) and six machine guns (including two anti-aircraft units). They went into service in the Balkans in the latter half of 1944. After the winter of 1944-45 three more so-called armored pursuit railcars (No. 51-53) were built, which were equipped as were Railcars No. 18-23 (but looked different), except for having, instead of two rotating turrets with 7.62-cm cannon, those of Panzer IV/H with 7.5-cm KwK L/48 guns. They were finished at the factory, but probably never went into service.

The individual cars of Type BP 42 armored trains. Right: the tank-carrying car. The Praga 38(t) tank was in a lowered area, which, along with the additional side armor, protected the entire running gear. The loading ramp was fixed in place, and the pusher car running in front of it was cut off to match. Below: the Series 57 armored locomotive with the auxiliary tender (to increase the coal and water supply and thus the range). The emblem of the rising sun on the tender is the symbol of the Armored Train No. 63. Lower right: Officers get into the command car. These carried not only the tactical and intelligence troops and medical corpsmen but also part of the infantry crew. In the middle is a raised, armored observation post with a searchlight; frame and staff antennae for the radio system are on the roof. Every train had a second such car as a spare, which served to house the infantry crew. (3 x vA)

Below: Every standard armored train had two Panhard 38(f) scout cars as reconnaissance vehicles; they were usable on the road as well as—after removal of the rubber tires—on the tracks (though the road tires could not be carried along while traveling on the rails). Right: The artillery cars of the BP 42 armored train. Above: the cars that followed the tank carriers had 7.62-cm F.K. 295 l/(r) guns and a raised mount for the quadruple 2-cm anti-aircraft guns. Below: the cars running before and behind the locomotive, with the 10-cm light F.H. 14/19(p) guns. In the other half of the train they carried part of the infantry crew. (3 x BA)

The same cars in Armored Train BP 44. Most noticeable is the replacement of captured Russian and Polish guns with 10.5-cm light F.H. 18 M of German manufacture, which now were the sole, complete armament of the armored trains. Otherwise, the other cars of BP 44 (tank-carrying car with Skoda 38(t), command car, locomotive) showed only minor changes compared to those of BP 42, for instance, in the formation of the machine-gun ports with two-part closing hatch covers, now in somewhat different form and built directly into the armored wall, while in BP 42 they were in riveted-on panels (compare the changes in the angled corners of the wagons of BP 42 and 44, and see the opened machine-gun port in the lower right picture on page 29, above the open door). (2 x BA)

The most important new feature of BP 44, though, was the armored pursuit car in place of the earlier pusher car. It held (above) the turret of a Panzer IV/H, on an armored base, with the long 7.5-cm KwK L/48, usually with additional armored aprons, that now gave the train an effective means of driving off Russian tanks. Note the plow blade in front and the angle in back (to make room for the tank-carrying car's ramp). The middle picture shows the front group of cars, which best shows the new appearance of the BP 44, of which the bottom picture gives a complete impression. (3 x BA)

Left: This picture of the anti-aircraft battery shows several interesting details: the partly folding breastwork, the window (A) in front of which an armored shutter can be pushed, the observation port (B, here open) that can be closed with a hatch cover, the closed machine-gun port (C) and likewise secured gun ports (D). (BA)

Above: A look at the radio cabin of the BP 42. In the background is the window with the sliding armored panel.

Left: The cars were linked by crawl spaces. At the far left is the crawl-space opening in closed and opened form (note also the armored aprons for the coupling). To form the crawl space, the panel before the door was folded down to serve as a floor, the panels hanging at left and right were erected as sidewalls, and the panel hanging diagonally over the door was closed from above. The nearer picture shows the completed crawl space. (BA)

Armored railroad train, light scout car.

Armored railroad train, heavy scout car.

Schematic drawings of the scout-car armored trains, planned in 1943 but only delivered to the troops in 1944.

Below: The armored train (light scout car) consisted of ten individual cars, identically equipped only with machine guns (left: half a train, consisting of five cars; right: an individual car), each car having a powerplant. The automatic central coupling enables a quick uncoupling of the train into groups or individual vehicles, and their reassembly. (BA/MA)

The armored train (heavy scout car) actually consisted of twelve differently equipped cars: two anti-aircraft gun cars, four artillery cars with Panzer III/N or IV turrets (short 7.5-cm KwK L/24; lower left picture), four infantry cars equipped with machine guns, and two command cars (lower right). At the ends of the train were tank-carrying and pusher cars. Lack of materials (the trains were finished only at the end of 1944) obviously made the completion of this plan impossible. The train on the picture at the side consists of only eight scout cars: the anti-aircraft cars and two artillery cars are lacking. (2 BA/1 vA)

Left: Of the 15 armored railcars built at the beginning of the war, only the last (No. 15), shown in this picture, remained in service after the summer of 1940, and even to the war's end. Its appearance lets one suspect the descent from passenger cars. (BA/MA)

Pictures below: Armored Railcar No. 16 was finished only in January of 1944. It was a new German design with a 1200-HP Diesel motor and the gun turrets used in BP 42, with 7.62-cm F.K. 295/1(r) guns. The lower right picture shows it with a pursuit car made of a captured T 34 tank, an interesting indication that not only the turrets of the Panzer IV were used. (2 BA, 1 Kr: Herbst photo)

Upper pictures: In 1941 and 1942 numerous armored railcars, with two 7.62-cm cannon in rotating turrets, were captured in Russia (left). The first of these powerful vehicles was put in service on the German side in December of 1943 (right), after appropriate rebuilding) modification of the turrets, new antennae and machine-gun ports); it became Armored Railcar No. 17. Whether all the identically equipped railcars, No. 18 to 23, were likewise captured vehicles or partly German copies, is not definite (BA).

Right: In 1944 the Italian firm of Ansaldo was hired to build nine Type ALn-56 armored railcars, such as it had already built for the Italian Army. These railcars were intended to be escort vehicles for the light scout-car trains used in the Balkans, but not all of them reached the troops before the war was lost. (MA)

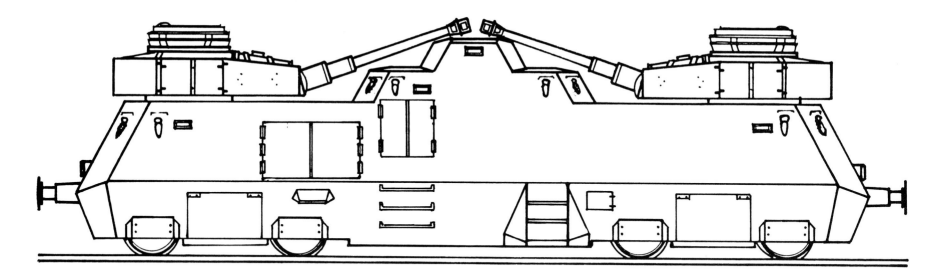

Above and lower left: An idea suggested in mid-1943 only became reality as 1944 became 1945—and then it was much too late: the equipping of an armored railcar with 7.5-cm KwK L/48 guns (in Panzer IV/H), which were strong enough for antitank use. These railcars (No. 51-53) were probably never put into service. (Sp)

Right: Along with the regular armored railcars, there were also those built by the troops themselves. Here is one such with a Russian tank turret and a 4.5-cm KwK. (IWM)

1943 to War's End

According to orders from OKH of July 17, 1942, the first six armored trains of the BP 42 type (No. 61-66) were manufactured, two at a time, in September, October and November of 1942. The first (No. 61) was ready for service in only four months and was turned over to the 201st Securing Division of the Central Army Group. The next two were also sent to the eastern front. No. 62 reached the Southern Army Group in February of 1943, No. 63 reached the 18th Army (Northern Army Group) early in May.—Meanwhile a critical situation had developed in the Balkans. The constantly increasing partisan activity became more and more of a danger to the main supply line of the German troops stationed in Greece, the Agram-Saloniki-Athens line. To be sure, Armored Train No. 6 had already been transferred from the eastern front to the Balkan area in the winter of 1942/43, joining No. 23 and 24, which had been in service there since 1941 and were already accompanied by five German and two Croatian auxiliary armored trains, but in the early summer of 1943, when Armored Train No. 23 had to be withdrawn for maintenance, this was no longer sufficient to secure the rail lines. For that reason, the OB Southeast received the next two armored trains (No. 64 and 65) in June and July of 1943. Further promises of the OKH could be kept only after long delays (the four light scout car trains intended for the Balkans arrived only from March to June of 1944) or not at all (one more armored train had still been planned for this area by the end of August).

At the beginning of August 1943, the partisan fighting behind the Central Army Group, which was fighting hard against the Russians after the lost Battle of Kursk, had begun to blow up railroad lines, seriously crippling transportation and giving the situation a threatening new dimension. To be able to deal with this threat, not only was the last armored train of the first series (No. 66) sent to the Central Army Group, but so were the first two of the second series (No. 67-72, ordered by the OKH on April 27, 1943); No. 67 was ready for service by the end of August, No. 68 only in November.

After the German troops on the eastern front were pushed more and more into a defensive stance, another important task arose for the armored trains in addition to fighting partisans: corresponding to the other side's earlier experiences in 1941-42, they showed their good defensive battle value, thanks to their mobility, armor and varied and strong armament, as the Russian attacks were often aimed at breaking rail connections to the rear. As early as February of 1943 the Debalzevo—Sterovka line was constantly freed from penetrating enemy forces with the help of an armored train, thus keeping the Hollidt army unit's withdrawal path to Mius open at least part of the time. In view of such uses and the critical situation on the south wing of the eastern front, including the winter of 1943/44, it is no wonder that the rest of the second-series armored trains (No. 69-71; as for No. 72, see below) were sent to this sector of the front.

When the new Inspector-General's office of the armored troops, no longer subordinate to the Army General Staff and the commander of the replacement army (BdE), was created as of April 1, 1943, the armored trains took on a hybrid position. They were still regarded as part of the armored troops and, during manufacture, were subordinate to the commander of Armored Troop I in Insterburg, to whose zone Rembertov belonged, but the office of the Commander of Armored Railway Trains (formerly staff officer of armored trains under the general of fast-moving troops) remained with the Army General Staff, though with a high degree of independence. So he retained command of the armored trains in service on German territory (otherwise, BdE was in command!). In cooperation with BdE, he could initiate changes in assignments, send requests for equipment directly to the AHA and its In 6, and bear sole responsibility for stationing ready equipment. Training exercises, as well as the preparation of instructions, guidelines and other printed matter for the armored trains, which he directed at the direction of the Inspector General of Armored Troops. Only organizational matters and the utilization of captured material had to be handled via the Army General Staff, the Inspector General of Armored Troops and the Chief of Army Equipment and BdE. The Commander of the Armored Railway Trains was the former staff officer, Colonel von Olszewski, who remained until this office was abolished on March 31, 1945 (thereafter there was only an armored train report to the Inspector General of Armored Troops, prepared by Major von Wedel).

At the beginning of 1944 the number of armored trains had grown to 30. With the Northern Army Group were Trains No. 51 and 63, with the Central Army Group No. 1, 2, 21, 27, 61 and 66 to 68, with the Southern Army Group No. 7, 10, 11, 28, 30, 62 and 69 to 71, in the Balkans were No. 6, 23, 64 and 65, in

France No. 22 and 25, as well as No. 31, which was being rebuilt, and in the hinterlands for repair service were No. 3, 4, 24 and 26. At this point in time, two trains first disappear from the list: No. 5, taken out of service by the summer of 1940, and No. 29, crossed off on February 23, 1942, probably used to equip the very makeshift 26-31 series, being the only one with a Diesel engine at that time, rather than lost to enemy action. Here one sees the astonishingly tough survivability of this weapon. Many types of damage could be done to an armored train, whether by mining the tracks, direct hits or bombing, but usually only part of the train was damaged and, as long as the rail connections to the rear remained intact, the train could be withdrawn and repaired. Even the remains of Armored Trains No. 10 and 27, heavily damaged in the siege of Kovel in March of 1944, were taken back to Rembertov after being liberated, where the decision was naturally reached that rebuilding them was not worthwhile, so that both trains were finally written off. Only when an armored train was immobilized by failure of the locomotive, derailment, or track destruction as the enemy approached, did it have to be abandoned.

Such situations increased during 1944. In March too, Armored Train No. 69 was lost between Tarnopol and Proskurov, after it had been caught in a tank attack, shot up, set fire to and derailed. On April 4, 1944 No. 70 had to be abandoned in Rasdelnaya, as all rail connections to the rear were broken. But the greatest loss resulted from the collapse of the Central Army Group during the Russian summer offensive. From the end of June to the end of August 1944, it lost Armored Trains No. 1, 61 (with Railcar No. 17), 66 and 74 (after only a few days' service at Warsaw),

and during the same period, the Northern Army Group lost Armored Trains No. 51 and 67, while No. 28 and 63 were lost in the southern area of the eastern front. In September No. 3 was lost in Courland, No. 71 in Rumania, No. 32 (formerly No. 31) in France, and No. 304 (light scout car) in the Balkans.

These heavy losses could not be balanced by an equal number of new units. In the nine months of that year before the end of September, only three new armored trains were put into service: No. 73 (in Italy), 74 (soon lost) and 75 (which remained with the training department as an instructional train); there were also the four light scout car trains (No. 301-304, sent to the Balkans) and eight armored railcars (No. 16, 18, 19 and 20 to the eastern front, No 30 to 33 to the Balkans). And this was all, though large-scale new construction had been planned for 1944 (eight **BP** 44 armored trains, 16 heavy scout car trains, 46 armored pursuit cars (including new ones to be added to the BP 42 trains), as well as five armored railcars—and this figure was even exceeded by the units built in Italy). Increasing shortages of materials (the Ukrainian steel mills, whose products had been available for the building of armored trains, had fallen into Russian hands in 1943) and weapons, and of the personnel needed to man them, who were

needed urgently elsewhere on account of the constantly worsening situation, resulted in constant lengthening of the time between ordering, manufacturing and readiness for service. Such delays were surely exacerbated in the summer of 1944 by the fact that the armored train training and replacement headquarters had to be moved from Rembertov to Milowitz (near Lissa on the Elbe in northern Bohemia) at the end of July, as the Russians approached Warsaw.

To help the situation, the construction of armored trains was moved to the second-highest priority level (equal to "Panther" and "Tiger" tanks) in August of 1944—showing what importance was now accorded them!—and every attempt was made to obtain the needed quantities of steel. Still in all, the

Warning for the armored train! The crew goes from home base (left), to battle stations (right). (BA)

program had to be extended from 1944 into the first quarter of 1945, and parts of it could not be carried out at all. Thus only ten of the sixteen armored trains (heavy scout car) could be begun, the construction of two of them was cancelled in January of 1945, and only two were ready for service at the beginning of 1945. Only three of the BP 44 armored trains had been delivered to the troops by this time, the already existing Practice Train No. 75 as Armored Instructional Train No. 5, and No. 76, sent to the Central Army Group in Poland, the new No. 75 to the Balkans (as well as the track-guarding train "Blücher", rebuilt into Armored Train No. 52, which saw its initial service in Tilsit). The intended number of armored pursuit cars (46) was not reached by far; thus the reequipping of the older trains could not take place, and even several new types could only be equipped by BP 42 standards for lack of such cars.

Despite this situation, the remaining veterans of the early days, Armored Trains No. 2, 4, 6 and 7, were taken out of service in the last quarter of 1944. They were replaced by Trains No. 22, 24 and 25, which had been used previously to guard the shores of the Mediterranean, but had been made all but useless by the heavy air attacks of the Allies in France, often aimed at the rail network, and were now sent to the eastern front. But by the year's end there had been further losses: the Central Army Group had lost No. 21, the former track-guarding train R had been lost in the Carpathians, and NO. 301 (light scout car) in the Balkans.

The year of 1944 also brought an organizational change. Until now the armored trains had been turned over by the OKH to an army group or army, which would put it under the control of an appropriate subordinate unit in their area of command for its intended use.

Impractical assignments and a lack of understanding of the nature of armored trains by those in command had often hindered their utilization, made it altogether impossible or even contributed to their destruction. In addition, it proved to be practical for defensive purposes to make up a battle group of several trains, as had originally been done with Armored Train No. 10 but had been given up; this was done not only for the sake of increased firepower, but also for mutual assistance, for example, by towing away an immobilized train. To keep all of this straight, it was decided to establish regimental staffs to command armored trains in the individual army groups. Such a position (Commander of Armored Trains: Colonel Becker) was already established in Army Group F (Balkan) by January of 1944. On the eastern front, where the army groups obviously could not be supplied with such staffs at once, a flexible solution was decided on.

For this purpose, Armored Train No. 72 was divided in the spring into two command trains, No. 72a and b; in February of 1945 an Auxiliary Command Train II was added, and another such train, numbered III, in April of 1945. Along with the creation of these staffs, four command trolleys were built, as were two repair trains (No. 1 in July of 1944 for Army Group F, No. 2 was to be ready for use in October, but was only completed in 1945—if at all). Command Train No. 72a (Armored Train Regiment 1, Commander: Colonel von Türckheim zu Altdorf), went to Angerburg in August of 1944 to cover the OKH headquarters at Mauerwald after the Russians had come dangerously close to the East Prussian border, and in November it was sent to Army Group A (later Central) in Krakau. No. 72b (Armored Train Regiment 2, Lieutenant

Armored train number 24 in the Spring of 1944 on a shore patrol mission on the Italian Riviera.

An armored train of standard type BP 42, well camouflaged with evergreen branches, covers the advance of an infantry unit. (BA)

Colonel Günther) went to the Central Army Group (later Northern) at Blonie near Warsaw. In April of 1945 another regimental armored train staff may have been organized (for Auxiliary Command Train III). The staffs could be transferred when necessary, along with their command trains.

At the start of 1945, the armored trains were apportioned at the fronts as follows: Northern Army Group (Courland): No. 26; Central Army Group: Command Train No. 72b, Trains No. 5 (Instructional), 30, 52, 68 and 76, Railcars No. 21 and 23 (?); Army Group A: Command Train No. 72a, Trains No. 11, 22, 24, 25, 62, Railcars No. 18, 20, 22 (?); Southern Army Group: No. 64 with Railcar No. 19; Aroy Group F (Balkan): Trains No. 23, 75, 201, 202, 302, 303, Railcars No. 15, 30 to 38;

No. 65, coming from the Balkan area, was being serviced in Milowitz. This arrangement makes clear the concentration on the eastern front, between the Baltic Sea and the Carpathians, and in the Balkan area, but also shows a differentiation: while the more heavily armed regular armored trains and railcars (No. 18-23) were used on the eastern front for defensive purposes, the mobile scout-car trains and lightly armed railcars (No. 15 and 30 to 38), being better suited to covering areas of ground, dominated in the Balkans, where fighting against partisans and enemy troops lacking many heavy weapons (for example, in Bulgaria) prevailed.

When the Russian offensive began in mid-January 1945, the few armored trains naturally could not do much to hold the

eastern front, from which spare armored vehicles had been taken to help the Ardennes offensive. South of Warsaw, only Command Train No. 72a could avoid destruction; all other trains stationed with Army Group A (later Central) were lost. North of Warsaw the situation was different; here all armored trains were able to withdraw at first, even No. 76, which was under pressure in Samland, as their movement to the rear remained free for a time. At the beginning of February 1945, the armored train battle group "Vistula" was gathered in Berlin to defend the northern Oder front, commanded by Colonel von Türckheim (Command Train No. 72a). The replacement depot in Milowicz was only able to repair regular trains No. 65 and the new No. 77; otherwise the army had to use track-guarding trains No. 83 and "Max". The Inspector General of Armored Troops and the governmental Ministry for Armament and War Production quickly had the track-guarding train "Berlin" equipped with "Panther" tanks. When the Russians broke through to the Baltic, not only was Command Train No. 72a surrounded in Kolberg, but Trains No. 30, 52, 68 and 72b were cut off with the 2nd Army in the area around Danzig and were lost there in March and April.

At the beginning of January 1945 it was decided to finish only the armored trains that had already been started, because of the lack of materials. This decision cancelled Armored Trains (heavy scout car) No. 209 and 210. With the surrounding of Breslau, the main production plant for armored trains, the Linke-Hofmann Works, was lost. The last traceable OKH order for armored trains, dated April 5, 1945, assigned personnel to Trains No. 81 and 82, ended work on No. 83 and 84, but ordered the quick construction of armored pursuit railcars No. 51 to 53, the auxiliary Command Train III and the track-protection trains No. 350, "Moritz" and "Werner", which were promoted to auxiliary armored trains, just as "Berlin", "Max" and No. 83 (and perhaps others?) had been previously.

The last documented departures from Milowitz, in mid-February of 1945, were Armored Trains No. 78 and 79, which were sent to southwestern Hungary. To what extent Trains No. 80 to 82 and 205 to 208, still under construction, were able to leave Bohemia is not clear; though notations for No. 81, 205 and 208 (March/April 1945) suggest that they went into action. The listings also show the reappearance of No. 4 as well as a "heavy" armored train, No. 607 (both in December of 1944), as well as Armored Train No. 99 (built April 4, 1945!), about which no further documentation could be found.

If one can believe the two surviving lists with notation dates up to the end of April 1945, the following regular armored trains must have survived the end of the war: No. 5 (Instructional), 23, 26, 64, 65, 73, 75, 76, 78 to 80, 82, 201 to 204, 206, 207 and 303. But one must realize that in these chaotic days not all losses could be registered. Train No. 76 in Samland was certainly lost at the end of April, and the trains that were on the Oder front or near Berlin (Instructional Train No. 5, No. 65, and No. 75, which was transferred from the Balkan area in February of 1945 to protect the headquarters of the Inspector General of Armored Troops in Wünsdorf) could scarcely have held out until May 9, 1945 either. What happened in those days can only be guessed. Only a few of the armored

train crews in the last hours could have had the good luck of the crew of Armored Train No. 78. This train headed homeward from the front into southern Styria on May 9, but had to be abandoned along with a supply

train when it got stuck on the steep cogwheel section of the Erzberg line. Nevertheless, the men were still able to cross the Enns by road the next day and let the Americans take them prisoner.

Armored Train No. 71 in the southern sector of the eastern front. At right is an armored anti-aircraft train of the Luftwaffe (also shown below). These trains with their penetrating 8.8-cm guns were also a welcome help to armored trains when they cooperated. (2 x BA)

Two pictures of Armored Train No. 63 on duty. At left one can see the loading ramp extending under the pusher car. The second machine gun in the hull of the 38(t) tank has been removed and the port covered with a circular armor plate. Right: a machine-gun troop prepares to follow the tank that has already been sent ahead for reconnaissance. (BA)

This is why the water tanks often had to be filled from bodies of water underway, using pumps brought along for that purpose. The pictures above and below show such an emergency supplying of Armored Train No. 28. (BA)

Above: Locomotive maintenance caused a serious problem in Russia, as the coal was of poor quality and the stations with water supplies (as in picture) were rare. (BA)

Left page:
Lower left: Armored Train No. 28 in a not yet identified station in the middle sector of the eastern front. Beside it is a captured locomotive of the Schtsch series.
Lower right: Armored Train No. 51 arrives at a station in the Northern Army Group zone in the spring of 1944. (BA, St)

One of the main tasks of the armored trains in Russia was securing rear connections against partisans. Left: To make the approach of partisans difficult, and to create open space for shooting, the forests on both sides of the railroad line were cut back several hundred meters from the tracks. Lower left: Track-guarding train "Polko" approaches a post with captured partisans. Below: People without permission were banned from approaching the railway lines. A member of the armored train crew examines a captured suspect. (3 x BA)

Right: an armored train of the standard series passes a fortified house along the railroad line. Below: A sentry demonstrates the watchfulness necessary in partisan fighting: captured machine gun and hand grenades are ready to be used. The armored train in the background has been coupled with an important transport train for its protection. Lower middle: Armored Train No. 28 with a supply train, possibly for the 83rd I.D. near Welikije Luki in the summer of 1942. Lower right: Despite all security measures, the partisans succeeded all too often in cutting the tracks. Stop signals and red flags then warned the trains not to enter the affected areas. (4 x BA)

Armored trains were often called on to protect tracklaying in dangerous areas. Upper left: a track-guarding train with a 3.7-cm antitank gun guards gauge-changing work in the southern sector of the eastern front.

Above: Many hands had to work together to bring the rails to their places. An armored train of captured Russian cars guards the site.

Left: An armored train unit waits in the background until the construction unit has rebuilt a stretch of track damaged by partisans, using materials brought along on the train. (2 BA, 1 Po)

The next page shows additional pictures from the last months of the war. Above: an armored train makes a counterattack on a station taken by the Russians. Below: an armored train fires all its guns in a night battle against the advancing enemy.

The fate of the armored trains: From March 1944 on, this scene became more and more frequent: a Russian cavalry patrol examines a destroyed BP 42 armored train.

Below: Abandoned by its crew at war's end but otherwise undamaged, Armored Train No. 73 sits in the Yugoslavian-Austrian-Italian border area. (2 x BA, Po, Kr)

ARMAMENT AND CREWS OF THE GERMAN ARMORED TRAINS

Train No.	Officers	NCO	Crewmen	Pistols	Machine Pistols	Rifles	machine guns		Grenade throwers	Artillery	Anti-aircraft guns	Bicycles
2	8	33	126	66	13	101	22	4	2	2:7,5cm Kan.(t)	2:2 cm Flak	15
3	8	35	128	79	13	92	26	8	2	2:7,5 cm Vers.Gesch. I./41	2:2 cm Flak	15
4	7	34	136	69	12	108	18	4	2	2:4,7 cm Pak(h); 2:7,5 cm le.I.G.	2:2 cm Flak	15
6²	7	34	112	76	13	77	20	2	2	4:7,62 cm FK 295/l(r)	2:2 cm Flak	19
7	8	33	132	70	13	103	26	4	2	2:7,5 cm Kan.(t)	2:2 cm Flak	15
21	8	38	140	75	13	111	16	4	2	3:7,5 cm FK 02/26(p); 2:10 cm FH 14/19(p)	2:2 cm Flak	15
22	8	36	130	71	13	103	16	4	2	3:7,5 cm FK 02/26(p)	2:2 cm Flak	15
23, 24	8	33	125	67	13	99	16	4		2:7,5 cm Gb.Kan.(ö)	2:2 cm Flak	15
25³	6	30	98	77	15	60	16	1	2	2:7,5 cm Gb.Kan. d/28(t)	2:2 cm Flak	15
26-28	6	28	98	65	14	76	12+3			3 Pz.Somua S35 mit 1:4,7 cm KwK u. 1MG	2:2 cm Flak	15
29-31	6	27	95	52	13	76	12+2			2 Pz.Somua S35 mit 1:4,7 cm KwK u. 1 MG	2:2 cm Flak	15
27⁴	7	35	120	69	13	93	18+2		2	4:7,62 cm FK 295/l(r); 2 Pz.Somua S35	2:2 cm Flak	15
10a	2	13	62	46	4	31	19			2:7,5 cm FK(p); 2:20 cm FH(p)	1:2 cm Flak	
10b	2	13	62	46	4	31	19			4:7,5 cm FK(p)	1:2 cm Flak	
10cpl. + Driver/Baggage	9	49	158	113	8	102	38			wie oben	wie oben	24
51⁴	6	27	84	60	9	57	10+4		2	4 Pz.Türme mit 4,5 cm KwK(r) u. 1MG	1:4x2 cm Flak	14

All armored trains also had: 3 antitank weapons, 1 flame thrower; as reconnaissance cars 1 armored trolley, 1 rail cycle; as baggage cars: 1 boxcar (1.5-ton), 1 passenger car, 1 living car.

Information according to K.St.N./K.A.N. of January/February 1942, except footnotes 2. August 42, 3. March 44, 4. May 42; 1. Officers including 1 paymaster; light machine guns: number after + sign = built-in.

Note: Most early armored trains were frequently rebuilt and reequipped; Trains No. 4 and 6 as listed above no longer have their original armament of 2 7.5-cm cannon(t)? Anti-aircraft guns only after the spring of 1941.

As reconnaissance vehicles, some Panhard scout cars 38(f) and Panzer 38(t) were used later on tank-carrying cars. Armored Trains No. 26-28(29-31) were set up in June of 1941 with a crew of 1 officer, 5(4) non-commissioned officers, 16(13) men, 6 rifles, 4(3) machine pistols (tactical group, gun crews and technical personnel); the infantry had to be provided by the unit with which the train was in service. Later Trains No. 26-31 were expanded to the usual extent with captured Russian material (see particular data for Armored Train No. 27).

	Offz.	Uffz	Mann	Pistolen	MPis	Gewehre	le.MG	s.MG	Other weapons & cars
ARMORED TRAIN UNIT BP 42 (K.St.N./K.A.N. 2/1/43):									
Driving unit (+ medical & radio troops & baggage)	3¹	9	18	11	4	19	2+2		2 Panhard 38(f) scout cars with 1 2.5-cm KwK & 1 machine gun, 1 passenger car, 1 boxcar (1.5-ton), 3 bicycles
1st train (including shock troop)	1	9	41	32	5	19	8	1	see data below
heavy machine gun troop		2	7	6	1	3		1	
grenade thrower troop		2	8	6	1	4			2 8-cm grenade throwers, 3 antitank weapons, 6 bicycles
light machine gun troop		3	17	16	1	4	6		6 bicycles
engineer unit		2	9	3	1	8	2		1 flamethrower, 4 bicycles
2nd train	1	12	33	28	3	18	6+4		see following data
artillery unit		6	17	18	1	12	4		2 7.62-cm FK 295/l(r); 2 10-cm FH 14/19(p);²
anti-aircraft unit		2	12	8		6	2		2 quadruple 2-cm anti-aircraft guns
armored unit			4	4	8	2		+4	2 38(t) tanks with 1 3.7-cm KwK & 2 machine guns
Technical crew (Railway)	1	5	3	6	3	3			
BP 42 total	6¹	35	95	77	15	59	20+6	1	see data above

	Officers	NCO	Crewmen	Pistolen	MPis	Rifles	le.MG	s.MG	Other weapons & cars
ARMORED TRAIN UNIT BP 44									
(K.St.N./K.A.N. 8/1/44):									
Driving unit (+ medical & radio crew)	2	4	12	3	2	13			
Armored grenadier train:	1	6	41	12	7	29	4	2	See data below
2 armored grenadier units		2	22	6	2	16	2	2	12 bicycles
grenade thrower unit		2	8	4	2	4			2 8-cm 34 grenade throwers
armored engineer unit		1	9	2	1	7	2		1 flamethrower
Tank and reconnaissance unit		5	7	9	3		+5		see data below
Tank unit		4	4	6	2		+4		2 38(t) tanks with 3.7-cm KwK & 2 machine guns
Reconnaissance unit		1	3	3	1		+1		1 Panhard 38(f) armored scout car with 1 3.7-cm KwK
Armored train battery	1	6	17	10	2	12	4		4 10.5-cm leight F.H. 18 M
Armored anti-aircraft half-train		2	12	8		6	2		2 quadruple 2-cm anti-aircraft guns
Heavy pursuit half-train		2	4	4	2				2 tank turrets with 7.5-cm KwK 40 L/48
Technical crew (Railway)	1	5	3	3		6			
Baggage	1[1]	5	6	1	2	9	2		1 passenger car, 1 boxcar (2-ton)
BP 44 total	6[1]	35	102	50	18	75	12+5	2	see data above
ARMORED TRAIN (heavy scout car)									
(K.St.N./K.A.N. 9/15/43):									
1 Car: Driver (medical & radio crew)	2	8	9	13	3	6	+2		1 Panhard 38(f) armored scout car with 1 2.5-cm KwK
1st Train (infantry)	1	6	41	18	7	27	6+4	1	see data below
1 Car: Driver	1	1	2	2	2	1	+1		
2 Cars: Machine gun & grenade thrower unit		4	28	12	4	18	4+2	1	2 8-cm 34 grenade throwers
1 Car: Engineer group		1	11	4	1	8	2+1		1 41 flamethrower
2nd Train (artillery)	1	11	39	39	7	8	+11		see data below
1 Car: Driver	1	2	4	4	2	2	+1		
4 Cars: Artillery unit		4	16	14	2	4	+4		4 7.5-cm KwK L/24
2 Cars: Anti-aircraft unit		2	14	13	1	2	+2		2 quadruple 2-cm anti-aircraft guns
2 Cars: Tank unit		3	5	8	2		+4		2 38(t) tanks with 1 3.7-cm KwK & 2 machine guns
Baggage	1[1]	7	9	6	2	11	2		1 passenger car, 1 boxcar (2-ton), 2 bicycles
Armored Train (heavy scout car) total	5[1]	32	98	76	19	52	8+17		see data above
ARMORED TRAIN (light scout car)									
(K.St.N./K.A.N. 10/1/43):									
1 Car: Driver (+ medical & radio crew)	1	2	2	4	2	1	4		
1 Car: Driver (2nd half of train)	1	1	4	5	1	1	4		
6 Cars: Infantry		6	30	30	6	6	24		
2 Cars: Engineers		2	10	10	2	2	8		
Baggage		5	7	3		9			1 passenger car, 1 boxcar (1.5-ton), 1 bicycle
Armored Train (light scout car) total	2	16	53	52	11	19	40		see data above
ARMORED RAILCAR:									
Armored Railcar No. 15	1	8	17	12	3	11	6		1 bicycle
Armored Railcars No. 30-38 (Ansaldo ALn-56)		7	23	13	9	8	2+6		2 tank turrets with 4.7-cm KwK & 1 machine gun, 1 grenade thrower
Armored Artillery Railcars No. 16-23	1	8	12	10	3	8	2		2 7.62-cm FK 295/1(r) or 2 10-cm FH 14/19(p)
Armored Pursuit Railcars No. 51-53	1	8	12	10	3	8	2		2 tank turrets with 7.5-cm KwK L/48, 1 bicycle

1. Includes 1 paymaster, 2. or 4 7.62- or 10-cm guns; light machine guns: number after = sign + built-in.

GERMAN ARMORED TRAINS OF WORLD WAR II IN CHRONOLOGICAL ORDER

Train No.	Ordered	Ready	1941[1]	1.44	12.44	1945	Abandoned	Notes
1	26. 8.39	16. 9.39	M	M			14. 7.44	+27.6.44 Bobruisk
2	8. 9.39		M	M			2.11.44	a.D. ?
3	5. 7.39	25. 8.39	H/M	H/M			12.10.44	+9.44 Gumbaikiaj
4	11. 8.39		S	H/M			18.12.44	a.D. ?
5	8.39						27. 7.40	a.D.
6	26.10.39[2]		N	B			12.10.44	a.D. ?
7	1. 8.39		S/H	S/H			20.12.44	a.D. ?
21	10. 6.40	22. 7.40	F	M			17.11.44	+10./11.44 Moscheiken
22	10. 7.40		F	F	A	M	4.45	+11.2.45 Sprottau
23	19. 6.41[3]		B	B	B	B		z
24	19. 6.41[3]		B	H/I	A	A	26. 1.45	+bei Krakau?
25(ex 9)	10.12.41[3]			F	H	A	26. 1.45	+13.1.45 bei Kielce
26	1. 6.41		N	N	K	K		z
27	1. 6.41		M	M			5. 4.44	a.D.n.s.Besch.b.Kowel
28	1. 6.41		M	H/S			15. 7.44	a.D.n.s.Besch.Karpaten
29	1. 6.41		M				23. 2.42	a.D. ?
30	1. 6.41		N	S	M	W/O	27. -3.45	+3.45 Gotenhafen
31(sp.32)	1. 6.41		F				11.10.44	+8.9.44 St. Berain
10	1.12.41	2. 1.42	S	S			22. 5.44	a.D.n.s.Besch. in Kowel
51(ex A)[4]	16. 6.42		N	N			28. 8.44	+13.8.44 bei Walk
61	1. 9.42	23.12.42	M	M			14. 7.44	+27.6.44 Bobruisk
62	1. 9.42	11. 2.43	S	S	A	A	26. 1.45	+18.1.45 bei Tomaszow
63	1.10.42	1. 5.43	N	N/S			1. 8.44	+17.7.44 bei Krassne
64	1.10.42	18. 6.43	B	B	S	S		z
65	1.11.42	11. 7.43	B	B	H	W		z?
66	1.11.42	23. 7.43	M	M			9. 8.44	+30.7.44 bei Siedlce
67	15. 5.43	22. 9.43	M	M/N			20. 8.44	+bei Riga ?
68	1. 8.43	3.11.43	M	M	M	W/O	18. 4.45	+bei Danzig
11(ex 10b)	1. 8.43	7.12.43	S	S	A	A	26. 1.45	+19.1.45 Krakau
69	20. 8.43	8.11.43	S	S			24. 3.44	+3.44 vor Tarnopoi
70	16. 9.43	8.12.43		S			25. 5.44	+4.4.44 Rasdelnaja
71	16. 9.43	12. 1.44		S			13. 9.44	+Rumänien
R[4]		10. 2.44		S			20.12.44	?
301(le.Sp.)	16. 9.43	29. 2.44			B		20.12.44	+Balkan
302(le.Sp.)	16. 9.43	19. 3.44			B		3. 1.45	+Balkan
303(le.Sp.)	16. 9.43	14. 6.44			B	B		z
304(le.Sp.)	16. 9.43	22. 4.44					21. 9.44	+Balkan
73	19.11.43	17. 6.44			I	I		z
72a(Bef.)	20. 2.44[5]	15. 7.44			N/A	M/W	25. 3.45	+10.3.45 Kolberg
72b(Bef.)	20. 2.44[5]	16.10.44			M	W/O	18. 4.45	+bei Danzig
201(s.Sp.)	5. 1.44	11.11.44			B	B		z
202(s.Sp.)	10. 1.44	11.11.44			B	B		z
203(s.Sp.)	21. 2.44	18. 1.45				B		z
204(s.Sp.)	23. 3.44	6. 2.45				B		z
74	20. 3.44	15. 7.44			M	W	8. 8.44	+28.7.44 vor Otwock
75(sp.Lehr 5)	15. 4.44	15. 7.44?			M	W		z?
76	4. 4.44	26.11.44			M	N/O		vermutl. +4.45 Samland
77	1. 5.44	2. 2.45				W	11. 3.45	+?
205(s.Sp.)	4. 4.44	?				M	28. 4.45?	z
206(s.Sp.)	17. 4.44	?				?		z
207(s.Sp.)	12. 5.44	?				?		z
208(s.Sp.)	25. 5.44	?				?	28. 3.45	+?
27(neu)	15. 5.44						20.12.44	nicht fertiggestellt
78	25. 5.44	10. 2.45				S		z
52(ex Blücher)[4]	1. 6.44	1. 9.44			M	W/O	27. 3.45	+3.45 Gotenhafen

Train No.	Ordered	Ready	1945	Abandoned	Notes
209(s.Sp.)	14. 6.44			19. 1.45	Bau eingestellt
210(s.Sp.)	7. 7.44			19. 1.45	Bau eingestellt
79(beh.)	10. 7.44	15. 2.45	S		+ 27.3.45 bei Celldömölk
80	7. 8.44	?	?		z
81	16. 9.44	2.45	M	14. 4.45	+ Böhmen?
75(neu)	23.10.44	31.12.44	B/W		z?
607(schwer)	4.12.44	?	?		z
4(neu)	20.12.44	?	?		z
82	14. 2.45	?	?		z
83	16. 2.45			5. 4.45	Bau eingestellt
84	16. 2.45			5. 4.45	Bau eingestellt
99	27. 4.45				

February-April 1945: the following track-guarding trains were taken over: "Berlin", "Max", "Moritz", "Werner", No. 83, No. 350, as well as auxiliary command trains II and III.

Notes:
1. As of Armored Train No. 10: first service area 1942/43
2. Preparation 7/10 to 10/3/1939
3. 2nd period; 1st period 3/1 to 10/2/1940
4. Former track-guarding train
5. By division of Train No. 72, dating to 11/23/43

GERMAN ARMORED RAILCARS OF WORLD WAR II

Railcar No.	Ordered	Ready	Subordinate to	Where in service	Abandoned
1-14?	1939?				1940?
15	vor 3.40	?	Pz.Zug 25,6,304	F(42): B(43-45)	
16	27. 1.44	?	Pz.Zug 11, (63)	S(44)	8. 8.44
17	10. 4.43	7.12.43	Pz.Zug 61	M(44)	9. 8.44
18	20.11.43	3. 7.44	Pz.Zug 11	S(44/45)	26. 1.45
19	20.11.43	30. 8.44	Pz.Zug 64	B/S(44/45)	
20	20.11.43	17. 9.44	Pz.Zug 62	S(44)	
21	27. 1.44	10.10.44	Pz.Zug 52	M/W (44/45)	
22	27. 1.44	26.10.44	Pz.Zug 22	A/M (44/45)	
23	27. 1.44	17.11.44	Pz.Zug 25?	A(44/45)?	
30	12. 5.44	17. 6.44	Pz.Zug 303	B(44/45)	
31	12. 5.44	17. 6.44	Pz.Zug 303	B(44/45)	
32	12. 5.44	12. 7.44	Pz.Zug 302	B(44/45)	
33	12. 5.44	12. 7.44	Pz.Zug 302	B(44/45)	
34	?	11.11.44		B(44/45)	
35	?	11.11.44		B(44/45)	
36	?	?		?	
37	?	?		?	
38	?	11.11.44		B(44/45)	
51	12.44				
52	12.44				
53	12.44				

Abbreviations:

A + Army Group A (44/45 Poland), B + Balkan, F + France, H + Hinterland, I + Italy, K + Courland Army Group, M + Central Army Group, N + Northern Army Group, O + AOK East Prussia, S + Southern Army Group (including all other units in southern area of eastern front: A, B, Don, Northern and Southern Ukraine), W + Vistula Army Group, z + until war's end.